Old War

BOOKS BY ALAN SHAPIRO

Poetry

AFTER THE DIGGING

THE COURTESY

HAPPY HOUR

COVENANT

MIXED COMPANY

SELECTED POEMS, 1974–1996

THE DEAD ALIVE AND BUSY

SONG AND DANCE

TANTALUS IN LOVE

Prose

IN PRAISE OF THE IMPURE
Poetry and Ethical Imagination

THE LAST HAPPY OCCASION

VIGIL

Translation

THE ORESTEIA BY AESCHYLUS

Old War

Alan Shapiro

Houghton Mifflin Company
Boston • New York 2008

For Callie
....

For information about permission to reproduce selections from
this book, write to Permissions, Houghton Mifflin Company,
215 Park Avenue South, New York, New York 10003.

www.houghtonmifflinbooks.com

Library of Congress Cataloging-in-Publication Data
Shapiro, Alan, date.
Old war / Alan Shapiro.
p. cm.
ISBN 978-0-618-45243-9
I. Title.
PS3569.H338O43 2008
811'.54—DC22   2007052823

Printed in the United States of America

Book design by Robert Overholtzer

QUM 10 9 8 7 6 5 4 3 2 1

The author thanks the following journals, in which these poems or versions of them
first appeared: *Blackbird:* "Skateboarder," "Some" (published under the title "Anybody?").
Cincinnati Review: "Bower," "Outfielder" (published under the title "Misjudged Fly
Ball"). *Literary Imagination:* "Night," "Day," "Harvest," "Old War," "Prayer for a New
Home." *Maggid:* "News Conference," "Just" (published under the titles "Redbud Leaves,"
"Luck"). *Pedestal:* "Dog and Owner." *Pequod:* "Last Wedding Attended by the Gods."
Rattle: "People Get Ready." *River Styx:* "Open-Mike Night in Heaven." *Slate:* "Suspension
Bridge," "Egg Rolls." *Tikkun:* "How," "Breaking News," "Watch." *Virginia Quarterly
Review:* "Country-Western Singer," "Poet," "Dentist," "Family Man," "Where" (published
under the title "Questions for the Soul").

"Outfielder" (under the title "Misjudged Fly Ball") appeared in *The Best American
Poetry 2006* (New York: Random House). "Country-Western Singer" appeared in *The
Best American Poetry 2007.* "Listen" was first published in *Matzo Balls for Breakfast:
Reflections on Growing Up Jewish,* edited by Alan King (New York: Free Press, 2005).
"Old War" appeared in the Kingsley Tufts Poetry Gallery Chapbook.

The author also wishes to thank Joe Regal, Michael Collier, and all his dear friends
(the usual suspects) for help in putting together this manuscript.

CONTENTS

III

FROM *The Book of Last Thoughts*

I

OLD WAR

Where is the bower?
Inside what book
Beside which window
In an ancient city
I went to more
Than thirty years ago?

Where is the bower?
The bright mesh
Made from the names
Of flowers that I,
Beyond the page,
Could not identify?

Where is the bower?
The loosened tress,
The laugh, the eager
Rustle of the hand
That slips the thin
Strap from the willing dress,

And as it falls
The *Dear heart*
How like you this?
Plain courtesy
Of wanting what
Is wanted when it is?

And when the bomb
Exploded and
The window shattered
In a silver shower
As oddly pretty
As any in the bower,

A silver shower
Showering red
Over the words
That told how birdsong
Answered birdsong
Everywhere overhead,

And everyone
Who could was running
While the bloody page
Went fluttering out
Into the city
Where the old war raged —

Where was the bower?
And where is it now?
And how do I
Get back to where
The dress is falling
But not yet on the ground?

BOWER

Our bedroom in a small
house in an old
forest where trees
lean down over
trees around
this opening
that they enclose —

neither apart
from the world nor
altogether
in it, of it,
where what comes
to us comes through
what holds it back,

scrimshaw
of leaves on leaves,
the farthest stirred
by breezes we
can hear but
don't yet feel
through the open

window where
the drawn curtain
too is stirred
and lifted like
a breeze-shaped
vagrant boundary
set to make

what's coming in
to us come more keenly,
not to keep it out.
Shadow of leaves

commingling
with the single
shadow of our bodies

stirred and lifted
on the lifting
scrim between what's
near and far,
inside and out,
all held now
and slowly moving

toward the sudden rush
of downpour and
love cry becoming
birdcall sifting
in the plush dripping
of the downpour's
aftermath.

HARVEST

after Sappho

As an apple hangs
in a fragment of
a sentence in
an ancient poem
in the book
you've made me
turn face down
on the bedside table,
your blouse now half
unbuttoned as
the apple reddens
in the broken
simile the second
half of which
was lost how many
centuries ago;
as the apple shines
more brightly for the lost
lines in the top-
most branches, missed
by the pickers, or
too high for them
to reach,
        untouched,
unfalling, trembling
forever on
the trembling branch
beyond the out-
stretched fingers
while you shiver
slightly as the blouse
falls, first this sleeve,
then the other,
from your shoulders.

EGG ROLLS

The gregarious babble
muffled the sharp
words the couple
in the next booth
were trying all
through dinner not
to have;
                    only
an occasional
No you, you
listen for a change
or *How dare you*
or *I can't believe this*
                    would rise
above the barely
suppressed
                    staccato please-
God-not-now-
not-here rhythm of
an argument they wanted
both to swallow
                    and spit out.
Then the pause,
the momentary
silence in which
                    the whole place
seemed
          to be listening
to the woman say, at last,
clearly and slowly
so everyone could hear,
                         "It's not
the egg rolls, Harry,
it's the last ten years."

Oh, Harry, can you
forgive them,
            the young couple
in the next booth
who laughed out loud
but really did
try not to?
       Surely
you heard them —
how could you not have? —
as you ran past,
hurrying after her,
your disappearing wife?
And though it's nearly
thirty years
             since then,
would it console you
now to learn
they didn't last a year,
that couple,
       and even
that night,
       although
they strolled home
hand in hand,
a little less estranged
       for all the laughter
you occasioned,
even after
       making love
and meaning it and
lying back, no part
of either of them
touching now, they heard —
they couldn't help
but lie there wide
awake and hear —

the couple from the next
apartment,
                who
for all they knew
could have been you and her,
go at it longer
                louder
deeper into the night
than they themselves
had ever thought
was possible?

PRAYER FOR A NEW HOME

God of the left-
open mailbox
in and out
of which a mother
finch flew so
discreetly it almost
seemed she tried
not to be noticed,
which made us notice
and draw closer
to the faint cheeping
and dim hint
of hatchlings way
back in the dark
behind a berm
of moss and twigs;

God, too, of the mailman,
who, despite
the notes we left
him asking please
when he puts
the mail in please
don't shut the door,
would shut the door
so that each day
when we opened it
till the chicks fledged
the mother bird
would burst out
in a panicky
accusatory rage —

in the universe
of birds, our hand
identical

to his, protecting
and destroying
unaccountably,
unsearchably;

Almighty, stray
bullet of
what happens —
                    Silence
we call a deafness
in hope of being
heard —
            hear us, bless
this house, protect it
from the cruel
or accidental
depredations,
                    pity
such helplessness
as makes us think
we cannot do
without you, as makes
us pray to you
while knowing it
exaggerates our self-
importance even
to think you would
ignore the prayer.

PEOPLE GET READY

I couldn't tell you where the Lord was traveling,
only that I knew he was
by how the lightning
flashed under his footfall
the way a rail does under a wheel.
He was traveling on a rail of lightning
made entirely of souls,
and I was there
among them, I was one of them,
invisible, uncountable,
suspended moment in an endless line,
and when it was my turn
to flash awake
into my short existence
under the pressure of his heel,
I knew my anguish
was the very way he moved,
how he could get where he was going,
though what the purpose of his going was
I couldn't see.
I saw relentlessness, not purpose.
I saw how he went, not where.
And as he passed I saw
he no more thought of me
than a train thinks
of the sparks scattering
under its iron weight,
bright, then dark.

DOG AND OWNER

1

What's obvious is what surprises,

that the naked man
made to look like a dog
with dog collar and leash
looks more like a dog
than a man caught
in a sex game or
threatened with lynching
or dragged like meat
across the floor—
            a dog
who's just now
rolled in something,
something which so
engrosses him
that for the moment
of the picture he doesn't
realize he's been yanked
back.
      What?
That's what his look says.
             And the soldier,
who holds the leash as if
she were the owner of the dog,
looks like the owner of a dog,
her casual T-shirt tucked
into fatigues tucked neatly
into boots,
        dog owner on a morning
stroll, this morning
a bit distracted, thinking
maybe about the day
ahead or last night, what

she should have done, or did,
and so fails to notice
what the dog is doing
till it's too late
and she has to jerk
the leash hard
to pull him back,
letting his lead
go slack,
   the moment
of the picture when
you almost hear
her saying, stern but not
unkindly, Come on now,
boy, let's go, the fun is over.

2

The mind strains
to sniff the delicious
stink of outrage,
stink of pleasure
of not suffering
that, of doing
that, of being done to
that way.
   Irresistible
stink of the mind
that the mind strains
not to nuzzle
into, roll on,
lap up, the taut
leash jerking it harder
and harder.
   What?

BREAKING NEWS

The girl on the screen
is telling
              something,
eyes
        not looking
at the camera,
                    voice a babbled
drone, ghost town
of un-
        inhabitable
affect —
          difficult
to hear
        till it falls
faint behind the voice
of the interpreter
whose words obedient
and diligent build up
a tower around her
brick by articulate
brick
        till there is
nothing left
          to notice
as the lens widens
but the charred sandal
in the foreground,
                    how the breeze
blows back the smoke
still rising from it
so that it's running
                    toward me
as it runs in place.

NEWS CONFERENCE

Invisible slow tumbling drift of ash
over the smoking city sifting flake
by flake down out of the lethe of itself
in a freedom of dispersal beyond belief —

What was the lesson? Steam of whose rage?

particle of particle of dry
continuous blizzard of the long-extinguished
fires of what, in the name of what, now falls
as new flakes falling among the not yet nameless —

What were the numbers saying when they spoke for themselves?

over the hot hoods of the jammed traffic,
the flipped-up middle fingers of the late-
for-work, and horn blare, cry of sirens near
and far, but never farther never nearer

What shining city on what hill exactly?

over the weeping prophet's back as he bends
to kiss the footprints of the led-away,
and into the footprints, too, when he rises, till
there are no footprints, and there is no prophet

What call? What visionary dream? What now?

only the gate trampled, the rampart broken,
the smoldering bus, and shoe; only the soon
forever noiseless drifting of the ashes
of the exhalation of the long-exhaled.

SOOTHSAYERS

When the soothsayers speak,
The music of their voices is so
Melodiously earnest that you feel
It cannot be the music of their voices
Only but sincerity itself,

An ancestral "trust me" that is truer
For being no one's in particular,
Intoning that it alone remembers
The difference between
The gate of ivory and the gate of horn.

When the soothsayers see,
They see with a single keen
Eye slipped from its socket to be tossed
From seer to seer until the vagrant
Angles of their seeing blur

Into all that's seen,
And seeing substitutes for knowing,
Which is why, as the polling indicates,
We viewers watch and say,
I see, I see.

When the soothsayers write,
Their words float from the page
Like bubbles smeared
With such iridescences of cheer
That we forget we're being told

To lie down in a ditch
And wash with pigs' blood
Now, or else.
And if what they predicted
Doesn't come to pass,

It's only because it wasn't
After all what they predicted.
It's only because they're centaurs
In a room of men and horses.
When they pass each other in the street, they laugh.

LAST WEDDING ATTENDED BY THE GODS

How they loved us
was
      in leaf sheen
where no leaves were;

distillates of light;
poolings
      of sun glint
off wine tipped

from the lip of bowl
to cup.
      The way
water in a fountain

seems to freeze
while falling,
      fresh
as snowmelt,

radiant as snow, open
to our every
      wish
as air is

to our voices.
Love was
      the sensation
of the promise of

more love to come.
Nothing ever
      changed
until it did.

Then the corpse fires,
and the useless
                fires
of sacrifice and supplication;

then the recognition
that they'd
             turned away
from us as happily

as they had turned
to us
        before,
the desolate recognition

that love was no more
meant
        for us
than sunlight is,

falling as it falls
haphazardly,
              on
everyone, and we

for a little while just
happened
          to be there
in the way of it.

WE

the mud-souled, the fast-talking not-so-fast
deserters from the armies of the Big Idea,
the two-timing temporizers and connivers
on the hands-up frontlines of Operation What The Fuck,
the burning in the hands when the reins tear loose,
what the overseers overlook, the eternal not-quite-
contented malcontent dissenters from the Book,
the Way, the Wheat, the Chaff, the enemies
of the enemies of "And that's true too," of night
in the name of darkness, of snow in the name of white.

SUSPENSION BRIDGE

Inbound over the Mystic River,
V on V of girders out
the window, and beyond the V's
a smokestack gushing smoke that billows
hugely white against the darkness

and, even drifting, seems somehow
more solid than the span it drifts
across and swallows up entirely,
the bridge suspended from a cloud.
Sensation of war. Deployments.

Little lights along the catwalks
and ladders running up and down
the water towers near the shore,
and headlights shining into taillights
flashing on and off as far

as where the lanes converge and branch
off into ramps that cars swerve out
in front of other cars to take,
while other cars swerve out from on-ramps,
speeding or slowing as they merge.

Sensation of war. Of being mobilized.
Each urgent vehicle, each signal
and countersignal, flash of brake
light, finger reaching for the scan,
the tuner — all the too-small-

even-to-be-recognized-
as-small maneuvers of a massive
operation, effect of orders
being passed down through a steel
chain of command, from car to car,

from bridge to central artery
to boulevard and avenue and street
through the deserted civic heart
of picture windows that the headlights
soon will sweep across, sweeping

across like searchlights over
the momentary faces and torsos
of mannequins arranged like decoys
in civilian dress, in all
the postures of suspended living.

COLD

is the coin's amnesia of the hands
it's passed through on its way to here:
the trace heat of the hands is the tiniest
particle still orbiting within the smallest
atom of the coin stacked in the middle
of a roll of coins at the bottom of a floor-
to-ceiling stack of rolls along the back
wall of a bank vault underneath the bank
in the middle of the city — and the way
that particle is slowing to near stillness
is how the cold moves out from particle
to particle, to atom, through the coin
and roll and stack until there's nothing else
beyond a frozen currency of such profound
forgetting that your hand, your finger, your
capacity to feel at all, would turn
aphasic at the touch of it, burning with cold.

DAY,

       bright negative of night, dreamlike in the tentative
first moment of my emerging not from sleep
alone but from the lingering sense of breathless
scrabbling deep in the earth through a crabbed maze
of never-ending dirt I had to eat to get through
to get nowhere while somebody somewhere both
behind me and before me near and far
laughed out a reckoning that wouldn't stop
till day came, light came, and air, and you
beside me saying my name, which sounded
just then less like forgiveness than reprieve,
appeal, the sentence suspended a little while
while through the brightening the night withdrew.

BEFORE

you entered the room, there was just the room,
and all the soundless damage of the air,
its rain of invisibilities; before you entered,
before I noticed you were noticing
how sunlight angled down from windowpane
to floor, and how the merest particles
meticulously bright were raining through it,
briefly between the dark above them
and the dark beneath, before you entered,
before the sunlight seemed to fall more slowly
because you watched it fall through the wine glass
left all night on the table, and how the light moved
without appearing to from rim to glass
and glass to bottom where it turned the faintest
streak of dried wine to a drop of fire
in a pool of light before it turned it back.

LUCK

My hand on you,
your hand on mine.
Your hand on mine
too light to guide
it as it lolls
in eddies down
from underarm
and over rib
cage to the curving
in of waist
and out of hip
and in and out
               too light
to hold or guide
it, hardly touching
it at all
but touching it,
unable not to,
as if in dis-
belief, as if
it wouldn't be
there if you didn't
touch it — even
as your back arches,
and the cry
you cry then is
the opposite of grief.

EASY STREET

Pompei

A thousand years from now
They'll dig us up. They'll find us
Here like this, like anyone.
They'll hurry to copy
Down the words
Before the plaster crumbles
At the touch of air

Raining ashes on the words
Someone not as lucky
In love as we were
Scrawled on the wall
Outside our window
Along the Via dell'Abbondanza.
"Passion runs off like rain."

Rain coming on so suddenly
That we stop to listen,
Holding each other,
A couple suddenly entombed,
For all we know,
Beneath a rain of ash
From the exploding mountain.

II

SOME

dead thing's scent led me across the pasture,
into a drifting maze of early mist,
past where the horses graze, amid the horse
scent, scent of grasses, in the tall grass, faint
but never fainter, never less distinct.
Where is it? Is it there? And what? And why?
The day's first quiz. The day, fairest of teachers,
patient because at ease, with time to kill,
floating the questions, letting them hang in the air
while far away across the valley a dog barks
and a child is laughing, and higher up, the mist
burns down to thin smoke in the crease of hills.

NIGHT

of the empty city, of block on block of traffic lights
changing to no traffic above the intersections
of the avenue curving in the distance out of sight;
the thorough silence in which my brother eight years dead
was suddenly beside me, the surprise of feeling
no surprise that we were walking stride for stride
somewhere only the dream needed to know about,
the two of us happy together walking, happy to let
the dream know where; and then the sense I woke with
that someone else had been there, someone in the dream
I was supposed to notice but noticed only later
when the dream was over, someone more shadow than man,
more night than shadow, sitting in shadow, head bowed,
hands on head, weighed down by sorrow, but for what?
some covenant betrayed? an obligation gone unmet?
as David and I walked past and kept on passing, all
the way down the avenue as if we walked in place,
lights changing pointlessly from red to green to yellow,
and the man in shadow more alone than ever
still waiting there inside the flown dream's empty city —
waiting for what, I couldn't say now that I've wakened,
now that my brother has returned to being dead.

AFTER

the last scan's last bad news,
and the breakdown, and then
the bitter composure
in the hospital cafeteria,
settling our trays on the table
before the sky-blue wall
on which the giant Virgin Mary
full of sorrow held out her arms
to all of us; after we saw her,
our sister at the next table,
not someone similar
but Beth herself as she was
exactly, reading the way
she did, engrossed,
oblivious, the thick pre-
cancer brown hair falling
over her face tilted
over the book she held
in one hand while absently
the other fed her until
she gathered up her tray
and not even noticing
how we were staring walked
past us back into the afterlife
while the Virgin dolefully
looked on and in my brother's
variation of the old joke
said, "You're dying,
and the food is awful,
and the portions are small."

HOW

in the bedroom of the afterlife a phone is ringing
on a bedside table beside a bed whose sheet
is smooth as steel, the crypt-cold pillow unindented,
and how the absence of a blanket on the hard bed's
white sheet on which the pillow rests reveals
the cold's irrelevance, how nothing heavier
has ever lain down on it to disturb it than the blanket
that isn't there, the ringing of the phone that never stops,
and how it rings and rings is how the living call,
and how the dead reply is how it goes on ringing.

MIST

like ink in water, white ink in white water
rising as it drifts from the white page
of the spectral city in eddying palimpsests
of figures on the sidewalk forming
and re-forming in and out of one
another — brother mist and sister mist,
mist of no brother and no sister, of
the eye subsiding into mist, of the mute
mouth of the vagrant on the bench
at the bus stop, head thrown back, asleep,
the slack mouth open to a wordlessness
that's opening to it — mist twisting up
through manholes, out of iron grates,
from pipes and wheel wells, leaving little
ropes of mist all knotted up and blown
to nothing as the buses pass right through it,
everything and everyone a ghostly fuel
on which the white lights and the red lights
burn and die and burn and die. Outside inside it,
you couldn't tell a soul from the exhaust.

JUST

after the downpour, in the early evening,
late sunlight glinting off the raindrops sliding
down the broad backs of the redbud leaves
beside the porch, beyond the railing, each leaf
bending and springing back and bending again
beneath the dripping,
                        between existences,
ecstatic, the souls grow mischievous, they break ranks,
swerve from the rigid V's of their migration,
their iron destinies, down to the leaves
they flutter in among, rising and settling,
bodiless, but pretending to have bodies,

their weightlessness more weightless for the ruse,
their freedom freer, their as-ifs nearly not,
until the night falls like an order and
they rise on one vast wing that darkens down
the endless flyways into other bodies.

Nothing will make you less afraid.

BLACK

flickering between the white slats
of the porch railing I'm not tall enough
to see above, trying to see above
or through it to the slow train
of long black cars I didn't know
back then were limousines
behind a bright black wagon
I didn't know was called a hearse —
and then I'm lifted up, my mother
lifts me, and together we watch
the black parade go by, and it's all
so shiny that the sky and trees
and the porch itself, the thin
white slats, are floating on the
black doors, on the hood, the roof,
and even the blacker windows where
nobody's looking back at me
but me, my mother, she looking on,
me pointing at me pointing
from the black door and the blacker
window and now from the black back
of the final car that carries us up
the steep hill smaller and still smaller
till we're finally over it and gone.

I'm facing my mother in the cramped living room of her small apartment in Chapel Hill, North Carolina. She and my father have recently moved here from California. She's eighty, he's eighty-seven. He with his Parkinson's and macular degeneration, she with terrible arthritis in her back and hands — they have started over in a new place where, aside from me and my wife and kids, they do not know a soul. As my mother explains it to her few remaining friends and family, they didn't want me having to traipse across the continent to care for them every time something happened. Better for me to have them living here.

She's struggled up out of her recliner, panting from the effort, and handed me the list of groceries I should get, if it's not too much trouble.

"Wait," she says as I turn to go. "Wait. Use my car. Let it be on my nickel."

I tell her no, I'd rather use my own, her radio's on the blink.

"Take the keys," she says. "Take. How far do you have to go that you have to listen?"

The question pulls me up short, disorients me, thrills and annoys me all at once. It's not just the tinge of Yiddish in the syntax, but also the stubbornness masquerading as request, the double exposure in the tone of pride and need that suddenly conjures out of thin air the kitchen table in the old house in Brookline, Massachusetts, where the elders sat and kibitzed. I could be ten years old again, or five, or even younger, too young to count as company, absorbing without quite knowing it the secondhand smoke of their inflections and intonations.

I say it over to myself: How far do you have to go that you have to listen? I hum it, I chant it like a mantra, as if it were itself the music of my childhood, the verbal key to an immigrant culture that's nearly extinct, that goes on living in my mother's and father's voices, if nowhere else. I think of how my parents got here, of everything they had to suffer: not just the painful but inevitable losses that come with having lived a long full life — the death of parents, relatives, nearly all of the friends who once sat around that kitchen table — but the unnatural devastations too: the breast cancer that killed their daughter in 1995, the brain cancer that killed their son a few years later. I think of the unthinkable, what it would be like to bury one of my own children, and I'm amazed my parents have gotten here at all. What could possibly have held their lives together in the face of so much shattering?

My mother stares me down, her one remaining child, and says again, in case I didn't hear the first time, "So? How far do you have to go that you have to listen?"

Not far at all, I want to tell her. But I know it's not an answer that she wants. She wants I should only take the keys. So I do.

LATE

for David

light retreating to the woods' edge
into the trees near the window
where vague clouds of yellow and red
suddenly sharpen into leaves
the tree remembers for a moment,
while back in the woods the night
dissolves, through draw and hollow,
all the textured surfaces it touches

and my friend said that until
his wife didn't know him anymore
she raged and beat him to make it stop,
as if he were to blame that the ties
that tied the names down to the named
had loosened suddenly into smoke
that everything lifted up through
as it drifted away from what it was,

the way, perhaps, as the leaves now
dim and go dark, the room behind me
is floating before me in the window
like a ghost room haunting itself,
desk, lamp, and chair, the wall of books,
my own face hardly mine among them
looking back and wanting in
out of the night that's coming through.

TIME PIECE

Late afternoon: first day
after daylight savings
when the suddenly
earlier evening
makes the day feel
later than it is;

mind as the body
time assumes
so as to know itself

my daughter half turns
away in a confused
decorum
from our old embrace,
the girlhood body
she was at home in
now erupting
into womanhood,

so as to feel
the fresh sensation
of itself in time

so that she's nowhere
more like a girl, a child,
than in this
new way she's not,

its aspect clarified
by being altered

my father new to being old,
and all the older for it,
with his bent back,
his toddler's gait,

body of time

he won't go
into the dining room
because they're all
just a bunch of old
potato pickers —
why would I want
to eat with them?

the body time assumes

his face expressionless,
his half-blind eyes unblinking,
not recognizing me,
my daughter:
what the hell, he says
to no one, just
because it's crowded
in there doesn't mean
it's popular.

Bad luck, bad history:
the right arm shriveled,
the hand curled
in on itself,
unusable,
the crippled gait

I try hard
not to stare at
when I see him
in the playground
I walk past
every day,

out on the court
alone, his good hand
hoisting the ball
up, banging the ball
on rim or backboard
so that it bounds

away and he has to
lumber after,
the gimped leg dragged
like a ball and chain
across the blacktop
over and over,

indefatigable,
his voice announcing
the last seconds
of the game forever
playing in his head
that he's always winning.

Genetic damage.
Damage of history,
of shame inside

the pleasure inside
the pity of
not being him,

of being white,
and then the panic
the day he calls me over,
saying, Hey man,
can you help
a brother out?

Panic of borders
breached, of history
in the sour air
I'm breathing as I reach
into my pocket
for what he wants,

sour air of history
when he sighs,
and shakes his head,
and smiles at me
so wearily
without surprise

as if his days were
days of just
this kind of thing
to get through, to
put up with, saying,
Shit, man, I don't

want your money,
holding out to me
the wristwatch
he can't with one
hand, understand?
buckle to his wrist,

and could I do it?
and now I'm fumbling

with the frayed band
that I can't make
fit through the opening
of the metal clasp,

and so he talks me
through it, teaching
me how, the way
a father does,
teaching the child
something he'd better

learn, teaching it
patiently but
with a patience that
the tone says
isn't inexhaustible,
You got to slow

down, just ease it
through the slot
a little softer
like it wants
to go there on
its own, like that,

man, yeah, like that,
and it's done,
he's turned away,
he's finished with my
being anyone
of use, I'm finished

being useful,
and again the cocked
arm hurls the ball
up toward the hoop
and the fans go crazy
as the announcer
cries out three two one.

NIGHT BLOOM

Caught in a net of vines
and long leaves leathery,
speckled with rot,

in places frayed, eroded,
eaten away to veins,
the veins to mesh —

improbably tonight,
before my eyes,
the bud splits,

petal peels off unruffling
from petal and whitely swells
and tips over

under the weight of opening.
Papery dragon mouth
whose fire is fragrance

so dense, so palpable
you almost see it, rare
fire of a father's

love, of the little cutting
he gave you more than thirty
years ago,

and of the death, too,
he fell in love with and
in secret wooed

and, vanishing, became.
You run the flashlight over
the fringed lip,

down the bright moist petals,
under the leaf it hangs from,
searching, hunting,

more rapt, it seems, than anguished,
as if the only question
you could ask

tonight is How? How
could he ever have wanted
not to see this,

not ever again to see, to
breathe in, this insistent
blazing open

of the gift he gave you
long ago? How
could you not tonight

imagine he didn't know
there'd be no end for you
of longing for it,

looking at it, the beauty
always counted on
and unexpected,

fierce, and hardly any
trace of it in sight
come morning?

FALLING

the irresistible fantasy
from the thirty-first floor
of the Hilton, looking down
over the rail of the catwalk
through the vast atrium
to the fountain so far
below it looks
like a continuous
time lapse of a small
flower flowering out
into a flowery pool —
to yield to it, to
give in for once
to all that giving way
of air, and falling
through it head
over heels or
swanlike arms
extended hardly
heavier than the
watery echoes — to feel
for once such
absolute release
from the clenched rail
of what makes even
the fantasy too much
a loosening, too
much relief, as if
the impulse itself
for such a thrill were the
resistance to it,
grip tightening
with the very force
of leaning out so far
above the ever-
flowering water
on the edge of air.

WHERE

will you go,
little vagabond,
anonymous familiar,
my hardly mine
there is no mine
without?
                    What will you do
there on that
blindingly bright
or pitch-black
shorelessness,
stripped naked, witless,

down to the un-
ironic spark
of what within me
wouldn't get
what's funny when
the Buddhist monk
                    who orders
a hot dog says,
Hey, buddy, could
you make me one
with everything?
Even thin smoke,

hovering
a moment over
burning leaves
as it disperses,
bears in its vague
and vaguer
                    curls and rings
the curled or crumbling
leaf shapes that
released it, as if

remembering them,
or trying to —

but you, my restless
tramp, my rude,
ungrateful houseguest,
as you drift away
unfettered, wakeless,
                              lost
as snow in snow,
will you bear any
trace at all
of who it was
who let you go?

HEAT

is passing at the touch from the hotter
to the less hot and from the less hot
at the same touch now made hotter
back to the hotter now made less,
minute continuous exchanges
at the border, at the membrane,
at the cell, invisible current and counter-
current of water boiling into air,
air steaming into water, the tarred road
at noon in summer sticking to the stick
a child is sticking the tar with, everything
heating, heated, or in heat wants to get
out of itself, give itself away, give way,
the way flame rises as if to get free
of what enables it to burn, your back
or mine, arched, rising, nearly off the sheet
at this or that touch of fingertip
or tongue whose touch is soft as ash
descending to a smoldering bed.

and unavoidable, that's how you have to see it,
Annie said, that's what it all comes down to,
what the Buddha teaches: separation,
sooner or later, from parents, spouses, children
most of all, no matter what, so what else
is there to do except accept it, embrace it,
trying to say it as if saying it
itself could be protection or escape,
as if the foresight weren't the perfect foresight
between the knife cut and the cry, the siren
and the blue lights in the rearview; the clarity —
something other than that never-to-be-
prepared-for sudden moment when the friend
you're running toward and calling to, and now
are touching on the shoulder to turn around,
has turned around and is no one you know.

"NOW,"

my daughter on the swing explained,
"doesn't exist," and she leaned back
and kicked her legs out and swung
the swing up high and higher toward
the lowest branch whose tip bent
slightly as a finch alighted. "How so?"
I asked, and she said, "Well, Daddy,
because now is the past of soon, and soon's
no sooner now than it's just now,
which is then, which then makes soon
a not yet now, and now a not yet then."
She laughed, and the chain ropes
she was clutching leaning backward
tightened straight out at the apex
of the upswing, her tiptoes
each time closer to the branch
whose tip bent under the finch
when he was there, then trembled
for a moment after when he wasn't.

III

From *The Book of Last Thoughts*

PASSENGER

The Paradise Express is in the station.
Someone in a voice like mine,
but mine made strange
by coming to me from outside myself,
is saying, This is Paradise,
end of the line.

Outside the window there are multiples
of shadows hurrying in steam
along the platform,
dragging their sullen little bags behind them,
hurrying where, for what, with whom?
and then I'm there

among them, Mr. Baffled, Mr. Cunning,
Mr. Just My Luck, all multiples
of me as we
glide up the moving stairs beside a tide
of other people gliding down,
of others all

so beautiful as they descend, so tall,
so fresh, that as I rise I hear
from everywhere
the stranger with a voice like mine announce
that the Paradise Express
is now departing —

It's then I know I've reached my destination,
the last stop, when the harsh whistle
comes to my ear
by disappearing till it leaves me here
on the floor in the terminal,
under the giant clock.

NARCISSIST

What room is this? Inside what building? And whose?
Why the concrete floor, as in an outdoor shower
Or an underground garage,
Declining slightly from the far-off corners
Toward a central drain?
And why the stepladder beside the drain
And the cup of coffee on the top step
Still jittery with steam
Below a fist
Of wires punching through the ceiling?
Why the ripped-open
But unused packages
Of insulation piled
Like sandbags
Along the walls that are hardly walls
But half-done jigsaws of joists, laths,
Pipes, and beams,
Door frames with no doors in them,
The drywall mottled with moisture?

There is moisture everywhere,
Everywhere there's dripping and trickling,
Faint, insistent, steady, like a word
Repeated to the inattentive
Till it gets through,
Though it never gets through,
So it's always repeated,
Whatever it is the room is saying
To itself about the room
Within the room
That holds within it what is trying to get out,
Or in, something
Impossible to know now

Because the workers and their tools
Have vanished from the site
At just that point
In the project
When the beginning
Of being sealed up
Is identical
To the end of being opened.

COUNTRY-WESTERN SINGER

I used to feel like a new man
After the day's first brew.
But then the new man I became
Would need a tall one too.

As would the new man he became,
And the new one after him,
And so on and so forth till the new men made
The dizzy room go dim.

And each one said, I'll be your muse,
I'll trade you song for beer.
He said, I'll be your salt lick, honey,
If you will be my deer.

He said, I'll be your happy hour,
And you, boy, you'll be mine.
And mine won't end at six or seven
Or even at closing time.

Yes, son, I'll be your spirit guide,
I'll lead you to Absolut,
To Dewar's, Bushmills, and Jamison,
Then down to Old Tanglefoot.

And there I'll drain the pretense from you
That propped you up so high;
I'll teach you how salvation's just
Salivation without the I.

To hear his sweet talk was to think
You'd gone from rags to riches,
Till going from drink to drink became
Like going from hags to bitches,

Like going from bed to barroom stool,
From stool to bathroom stall,
From stall to sink, from sink to stool,
From stool to hospital.

The monitors beep like pinball machines,
And coldly the IV drips,
And a nurse runs a moistened washcloth over
My parched and bleeding lips.

And the blood I taste, the blood I swallow
Is as far away from wine
As 5:10 is for the one who dies
At 5:09.

I

The thoroughness of passion, how
it fills you up till the you in you
is gone, is the antithesis of me.
I as the antithesis of passion
is not the maiden in her watchtower
pining for rescue or release
but the watchtower itself, myself,
the last retreat, the highest chamber
of dry vantage when the flood rises.

O my unfilled, unfillable,
pronominal nothing of the self,
the jig is up; dying has turned
your pretty figure of a watchtower
into an elevator stalled
between floors in a house of horrors,
and you at last, with all your slips
and vantages, are only what
remains when space contracts and ceiling
lies flush with floor, and wall wall.

BRAWLER

After the chin music, and the dugouts empty,
and the players swarm the infield, chesting each other, shouting,
the crowd all apeshit, everyone juiced to see it happen,

even the announcer's *Uh-oh, this is trouble*
now a kind of code for *Oh boy, let it rip,* when
just as suddenly the near mayhem dissipates

to mere game, and the announcer says, *Thank goodness,*
meaning, *Too bad,* meaning we turn the sound off — and Hal says,
You know, to really hurt someone you're hitting in the face,

you have to aim not for the face but for some point in space
behind the head, and then punch through the face to that.
Which is exactly what I'm doing now

except the face keeps changing, kaleidoscopically
becoming father, brother, colleague, teacher, friend,
while I swing hard to smash it down into the face

behind the face, the face that differs from the face
I'm swinging at, the way a fad differs from a tradition,
and at the moment I'm nothing if not traditional,

strictly old school, each swing the certainty itself
of truth in hiddenness, hiddenness in truth,
although by now it really doesn't matter who

I'm trying to hit because the face hangs tauntingly
just there beyond my reach as I lunge and swing and fall
short of the ever-more-hittable chin and jeering mouth,

the eat-me nose and cheek of mentor, tormentor, you
little shit you, you motherfucker, I'm bashing air,
I can't connect, my arms now shrinking shrinking while

the rest of me grows huge with rage I can't release,
a *T. rex* of gigantic fury lashing his shriveled
arms out at the face that's laughing at the harmless

things curled up and puny as a pubic hair.

SKATEBOARDER

I was just eighteen
      When the first fit
Threw me from my board,

And ever since my life has been
      An afterlife,
Adrift in a regimen

I needed to reduce
      My life to
So I could live it,

My body slack on meds
      And thickening,
Moving the now diffuse

Vector of selfhood
      In a mime
Of will from Quick Stop

To café to restaurant back
      To Quick Stop,
Year after damaged year,

Slow walker over a ground
      Of trap doors
The slowness somehow kept

From opening till now,
      And now I'm falling,
And the thing is

I'm alive again the way
      I was before
When I was beautiful

At just that moment when
      The skateboard hangs, suspended,
Perpendicular above the ramp,

And somehow I'm riding it,
        Nearly parallel
To the ground, right foot

At the low end of the board,
        Left foot at the top,
Torso tipped forward,

Arm flung out for the shifting
        Momentary
Balance as I ride

The upsweep of the invisible
        Wave that
Holds me holding it

Right here, right now,
        Where it neither
Builds nor breaks.

RUNNER

I hate the up-
hill sluggish push
of it and downhill
pounding and
the long dull flats
that end in turns
that turn back into
straightaways
that every step makes
longer and duller —

like beating your head
against a wall
for the endorphin high
of stopping, except today
I don't stop, can't, because
I love how hating it
slows time down
till each stride is its own
unbearable forever,

and time's more like
a pool now than a river,
a pool whose glassy
skin of trees, clouds,
sky, the world entire,
my every step
is shattering
like a stone.

TRANSCENDENTALIST

The eye that sweeps
the ceiling above the bed
over and over
in its final moments
is not the eye
of my symbolic
seabird perched
on its little
shoal of time,
resting its wings
a moment, calm,
between a wilderness
of waves before it,
and behind it, "bound
and road-ready
to plunge on
into immensity
again,"
       but
the panicky
eye of the exhausted
seabird with no
rest in sight, no
little rock
or islet to
alight to,
just the wingbeat
failing in the
freezing refuge
of what it
otherwise would seek
a refuge from.

See how it
plunges on into

the planetary winds,
across a wilderness
of water, blind
and road-weary
between immensities.

DENTIST

Spare me the judgment seat,
the immaculate apron
with its little chains.
Spare me the old saw
of a tooth for a tooth,
and the pearly whites
of the good doctor
who brings the blinding
bright light down. Spare me
That eternal Novocain.
That leaden sheet.

I know the drill.
I know the joke
About the final cavity
I'm soon to fill.
                  Spare me.

BROTHER

The shitty job, the busted marriage,
and the bad heart, and now
the cancer —
            I know what you're thinking:
I'm no one's recipe for fun.
I'm the guy you think of
when you need to think
it could be worse. I'm the "perspective,"
the Bosnian pen pal,
the guy whose job it is,
whose gift really, is to make
the girlfriend realize
what it was she loved about her ex.

But the truth is,
if I'm not what you would call
A happy man,
I can't say I've ever really felt unhappy.
I'm like a happy man
with bad luck, someone who's chronically
okay if you forget
the big picture and zoom in
on the animal texture
of each living moment,
the sensation of it,
what it is.
            Even now.
Especially now.

Dolores says
if I loved myself,
I'd complain more.
I wouldn't act like I deserve no better.
She thinks if you're not showing
how miserable you are,
you must be hiding it.

And if you're hiding it,
you're even more
miserable than she thinks.

My sister suffers from what you might call
a positive outlook, a glass-half-full
type of gal who can't shut up
about the empty half.

She went out of her way
to buy the mash potatoes
'cause she can't bear to see me
waste away. It isn't right,
and it's bought anyway
with money she don't have,
so I may as well eat it.

But I don't answer, don't
open my mouth. I'm looking
at one little crooked
gray hair on my right knuckle,
watching it quiver in the cool air
the little plastic fan is blowing,
the fan she always pulls
out of her bag
and places on the tray
between us 'cause it's so damn
hot in here, boy, how can you stand it?

I just keep looking at my hand,
my knuckle. I still have feeling there.
That's where my life is.
What it is. There.
There on that knuckle where
if it's cool, it isn't cold.
If it's hot, it isn't hotter.
The little gray hair quivering
happily as if nothing could be better,
as if to say, What more is there to want?
Dolores beside me holding the fork

against my closed lips,
forgetting she holds it there,
asking me if I think she's maybe
a little overweight
'cause when the cashier
handed her the tub
of mash potatoes, he said —
the little shit — you want a fork with that?
And she, like, told him, Do I look
like I'm gonna eat this
by myself, motherfucker?
And he's like,
                    I don't know your life, bitch.

FAMILY MAN

I stopped beyond the pasture
in the dark crease
between hills that rose
on either side
so steeply that
the only light left
was in the tops of trees.

I stopped where the snow
I had to stomp through
not to slip on
wouldn't break,
bracing myself
against rough bark
to keep from falling,

while over me
where the light was
there was wind
I couldn't feel,
that couldn't reach me,
the highest branches
pitching the last leaves

down through the shadowy
blue and bluer
stillness which
they deepened somehow
by disturbing.
Even my breath,
as I breathed it,

seemed to freeze
in the angelic
shape of its release.
And so, dear ones,

when I heard my name
come over the field
behind me where

the day was,
out of the alien
day, keen scented,
loyal, determined
not to leave
without its prey,

forgive me if
I let myself,
just then, be something
no name could find.
I was cold
and numb, and it was
sweet to be so.

HANDLER

All of the pokey small-town chicken-shit
scratching in the chicken-yard dirt
for power —

the public left hand conserving this
so that the private right hand
could develop that

while sweeping the ever-gathering homeless
under the downtown
welcome mat —

the gerrymandered and the jury-rigged,
the zoned, oh, we were good at it,
weren't we, Mr. Mayor,

your honor, you and I, we were
some team, never defeated,
never caught.

Our foreplay was the ploy
of values, the clean
façade

of straight talk, and the flashing
ordinances that passed
in looks

between us in the council
chambers and before
the press.

We sought the sly impolitics
of love under the table
like a kickback.

Oh, some of course suspected,
we had our enemies,
ex-wives, ex-

friends, and even the ex-
exes who had to pass
for friends.

Daily there were deals to broker,
palms to regrease,
and files, so

many files to open and keep open
— I kept meticulous files —
I managed all of it

for you, sir, I managed everything,
I who now can't manage
to move or speak.

If you could only see me here,
if you could visit — though
I know you won't,

you couldn't — what handler now
would let you? — but if
you could slip in

some night when hardly anyone's
on duty, and could see
my nurse,

my handler, my chicken come home
to roost, I think the vision of her
would amuse you,

hymning her righteous ha-ha — I'm saved,
you're not, O Jesus my
loving savior —

while she washes down my body
in that rushed half-assed
why-bother

way of hers that leaves my legs exposed,
the johnny bunched up
around my thighs,

and the catheter, my last cocksucker,
running out from beneath the
covers shamelessly.

MAYOR

I'm thirsty, and there's this dribbling down my chin.
I think I'm crying. But how could I be crying
When I cry and no one comes, and I'm still thirsty,
Angry and thirsty, and there's still this dribbling?

Where are my people? My staff?
Who shrunk the circumference of my power
Into the strap that's strapped the furious
Baby to his highchair in an empty house?

LANGUAGE

Some time after the neighbor died
and the house emptied,
you were awakened
in the dead of night
by the howling of his pudgy, half-blind,
arthritic beagle, who
had found his way home
from wherever he'd been sent to
and now was sitting before the front door
with his head raised nearly back
behind him howling and keening
to the vacant house
to be let in.

And is that how it will be for me,
your loyal little dog
of language, best friend,
beloved stray,
when I return too late
to the abandoned home
in the deserted neighborhood,
wagging my tail of words,
and then not wagging it
when I realize
that the door is bolted
and no one's answering
or even anywhere in hearing
to take away
the godforsaken howling?

OUTFIELDER

Just before he died,
when Tim had come back
from his dream of dying
to tell us it was all
just bush league, little league,
why the hell did I waste
time fearing it? I thought

of that moment when the ball's
hit and you start in and,
uh-oh, should have gone
the other way and all
you can do is watch it arc
over your clumsy scramble
to reverse direction —

too late, too late, why
hurry? And anyway,
isn't the lifelong
fought-against sensation
of defeat now nearly
irresistible, a sweetly
growing spaciousness

in which the celebration
at home plate shrinks
to nothing, and the cut-
off man, no longer shouting
or waving, turns away
to kick his glove in tiny
dust clouds down the infield?

POET

I was the one dead inside the music —
my voice forever in the cave of it,
shaping the quick clay

of syllables into songs of praise.
I was the one dead inside the praise
that praised you, "singing your praises."

I was the one dead inside the singing,
the one dead inside the song
I pulled away from you to sing,

withdrawn inside it, hiding inside it,
inside it touching you and being touched
inside and out, and knowing it all

only as melody in which
nothing exists beyond the wish
that if I couldn't love you better,

I could at least keep singing
as if I could. And all for what?
That last infirmity?

My voice forever scattering
away in echoes other voices
I will never hear might sound?

What good will it do me then?
That ancient story, love,
you know how wrong it is,

how backward, for it was you
who sought me out among the singing shades,
who turned back, and kept turning

daily, nightly, and I who vanished,
turning away from you
to listen to them sing

about how beautiful you are,
how stupid one would have to be
to turn away from beauty such as yours.

What wouldn't I give to touch your body now?
That's what the dead are singing.
That's what they've always sung.

All the dead know how to do is sing.

OPEN-MIKE NIGHT IN HEAVEN

I may be dead
but I'm dying here
among these not so
friendly Caspers
with their laundered
visages all mute,
blank,
        unkillable.
So I say, You know,
it's hard to do standup
when you haven't
got a leg to stand on.

Which gets me nothing,
not even a faint
hosanna of a heckle.

Anybody here from limbo?

But seriously, spooks,
where's the material in spirit?

I miss my body, I miss
your body — well, maybe
not *your* body;
        I miss
the cockamamie in-
between of having
and being a body,
the neither in nor
out of it — see,
that was my mother lode,
and man, what a load I was.

Yeah, I was so fat
I crushed my inner child.

My wife said, Honey
can I help you
off with that?
And I was naked.

I told her I needed
something looser to wear.
She said, How 'bout Montana?

Christ, if she hadn't
been a restless sleeper,
I'd have had no sex at all.

I loved what I hated.

I loved my girlfriend.
She was a ball-busting feminist,
so I never cheated on her,
not even with my wife.

She said she was writing
a kids' book about my penis.
What are you gonna call it,
I asked, *Hop on Pop*?
No, she said, *The Little
Engine That Couldn't*.

Speaking of the body,
I loved its leaky
stinks and secretions,
its sly reversals,
                    spinach
in the teeth of being cool,
the banana peels of dignity.

I loved my misery, and yours,
especially yours.
                    For the truth is
deprivation was for me

what gold lamé
was for Liberace.
            If I could wring
a punch line from the pain,
then for that moment,
anyway, I was like, what?
If not like you, Lord,
lordly.
        Which reminds me
of my Aunt Ethel,
a survivor, Lord,
who told me, she said, Sonny,
vhen I got out of Auschwitz,
I veighed sixty-nine pounds —
sixty-nine pounds and
I still had a fat ass.

O you who made
the fucked sprawl
of unbearable sorrow
we call talk radio,

who made *hog*
rhyme with *synagogue,*

and who alone knows
why Muammar Qadhafi
would take over a country
and declare himself
not generalissimo, not king,
but colonel?

What am I doing here?
You wise guy, you, you
Holy Trinity of stooges,
what's the big idea?
Why have you brought me
to the edge of heaven

if not to look back
to the infernal regions

(how infernal? *Don't ask,*
my aunt would say —
that is, Dantesque)

into the smoke-filled clubs,
the dives, the mine shafts
of the lower circuits,
where the ones
you're eternally killing
make howls that
from this distance sound
almost like laughter.

NOTES

"Old War": the phrase "Dear heart, how like you this?" is from Sir Thomas Wyatt's poem "They Flee from Me That Sometime Did Me Seek."

"People Get Ready": this poem is an adaptation of a dream quoted in William James's *Varieties of Religious Experience.*

"Easy Street": the quoted line "Passion runs off like rain" is an adaptation of Stephen Bertman's translation of "Impermanence" (Corpus of Latin Inscriptions, 9123), in the anthology *Erotic Love Poems of Greece and Rome* (New York: New American Library).